LAUGHTER IS THE BEST SUPPLEMENT FOR YOUR PSYCHIATRIC MEDICINE

This book is not intended to make fun of people with mental illness; it was written by people who have been diagnosed with various types of mental illness.

We hope to address the stigma of mental illness by letting the public know that we are not violent. We are caring people who work when our symptoms are less severe.

Created by Aras & Carmel, with contributions from Mary Hom, Andrew White, Michael Buckly, and Connie Bee

Illustrated by J Driver

Copyright© 2004 Aras & Carmel

ISBN 0-9759694-0-4
Library of Congress Control Number: 2004109898

Juxtaflux Books
9613C Harford Rd.
Baltimore, MD 21234

Acknowledgments:

We would like to thank the following people for their support:

Therapists, Barbara and Norm; Nurse, Karen; Psychiatric Nurse, Chet; Vocational Rehabilitation Counselor, Karen; Psychiatrist, Dr. Onyike; Case Manager, Evie; Medical Doctor, Naomi; and, our friends Isabel, Hillary, Sue, Isiah, Denise, Joan, Jana, Mary, Andrea, and especially Jesse.

Special thanks to our Editors Estela and Denise.

Also we would like to thank our former health care workers who have helped us to come up with jokes about cold-hearted therapists.

Introduction:

Although many of the situations are based on our realities, we used all fictitious names to protect the innocent and to prevent the guilty from suing us.

A joke or two a day might just keep the men with straight jackets away, unless it is highly inappropriate, then it might attract them.

We've designed the book so you have a chance to guess the answers to the riddles. You won't accidentally see the answer, because it's on the next page.

Laughter Is The Best Supplement
For Your Psychiatric Medicine

Dr. White: You know how I have all kinds of people on my case load?

Dr. Patall: Yeah.

Dr. White: And some of them are therapists themselves.

Dr. Patall: Right, so?

Dr. White: Well one of my patients was describing the trouble she was having with one of her patients. And the more she described this person, the more it sounded like Dr. Dickens, my therapist. It turns out that my client's client **is** my therapist. It is the same scenario for all 3 of us, we give therapy to our therapist's therapist.

How did the psychiatrist feel after he used E C T on himself?

Shocked.

Did you hear about the grandmother who flew from Florida to Maryland to see her grandchildren for Easter and her luggage was lost? She had packed Easter baskets full of candy for them.

Well she found her suitcase in a psychiatric hospital. It had been placed there because it was a "basket case".

Why did the therapist feel like a trash can?

Because everyone dumped their problems on her. But that's okay because half the clients thought that therapy was garbage that didn't work.

How did the news anchor man feel when he got his suit wrinkled right before his job interview?

The same way he felt when he lost his last job, de-pressed.

One psychiatrist asks another, "Should we call the people who see us patients or clients?"

The secretary interjects, "Considering they have to wait to get an appointment, wait to be called backed to your office, wait to get their prescription filled, and then wait to see if their insurance will pay, I think you should call them patients."

Why did the creature from outer space go to see a therapist?

Because he felt alienated.

Patient: This is bull, I'm taking my but on home!

Therapist: Take the rest of you home with it.

Why was the gymnast put in a psychiatric hospital?

Because she flipped.

Five reasons to let you know when it's time to get a new therapist:

1) When you catch a glimpse of her note pad and see a caricature of yourself with a big mouth and a caption reading "Yap, yap, yap…"

2) You find out she is a best selling author, and her book is about you.

3) You ask your therapist for a hug and she says she doesn't hug clients, but two weeks later you catch her hugging the patient before you.

4) Your therapist is running so late that the next client comes in before you are even called back to the room, you get to talking and it turns out she is charging you $50 more per visit than the other patients.

5) You were wandering why it always seemed like your 45 minutes were up so fast when you finally discovered that your therapist had a remote control device that sped up the office clock.

I was so mad at my therapist that when I got home I paged her with the number to the weather.

Why did the hit and run victim go see a therapist?

She was feeling run down.

The priority of professionals in the psychiatric field is to assess whether or not the patient's life is in danger.

However, most people feel there are worse things than death, especially people with phobias. For example, it is well known that the fear of speaking in public is more common than the fear of death.

Dr. Dickens, receives an emergency page from a client, while he is making love to his wife. He quickly calls back, but eager to get back to what he was doing, he asks, "Is this a life or death matter?"

"Oh no," replies the patient, "it's much worse than that."

Why did the dictionary go to see a therapist?

Why did the computer go to see a therapist?

The dictionary went to therapy to find the true meaning of life.

And the computer went to process its past.

What did the psychiatrist say after telling the patient that his session would be free?

He said, "Psyche. You got to pay."

Dr. Patall: I'm never going to see a therapist!
Dr. White: A therapist who won't see a therapist; what will you do about all your problems?
Dr. Patall: I'll go to the cleaners, they'll be able to shrink a shrink.

Why won't a cold-hearted psychiatrist take on a book for a client?

Because he doesn't want to get paged.

Why did the recovering alcoholic go to live on a horse farm?

Why did the travel agent need substance abuse counseling?

The recovering alcoholic's counselor told him he needed a stable environment.

The travel agent kept tripping.

Why did the slice of bread go to A.A.?

He got toasted.

How did the man with drug addiction feel after he burned all his bridges?

He felt like he had no way to get over it.

Why did the alcoholic take his wall with him to rehab.?

Because the wall kept getting plastered.

Why did the rehab. center allow the musician to bring his guitar with him?

Because the guitar was strung out.

Why did the guitar need trauma therapy?

Because his owner kept picking on him.

Why did the nail have to go for long term psychological treatment?

Because it had been traumatized by a hammer.

Why did the nail go to a sex therapist?

Because it wasn't capable of screwing.

Why did the photographer have to see a psychiatrist?

Because he snapped.

Why did the camera have to see a sex therapist?

Because he kept flashing people, there was way too much indecent exposure.

A TV and a remote control went to couples counseling:

The TV said, "She keeps trying to change me!"

The remote control said, "He never turns **me** on."

Why did the rooster need sex therapy?

Because his cock-a-doodle didn't.

Mr. and Mrs. Muddles in couples counseling:

"The way he treats me, makes me feel like an old sock!"
said Mrs. Muddles.

"Darned woman!" said Mr. Muddles.

"He's always trashing me," she added.

"Would you listen to this garbage!" he retorted.

What happened when the skunk's girlfriend asked him to go to couple's counseling?

He made a big stink.

Two math books were in couple's counseling.

He said, "I can't figure her out."
She said, "He's got problems."
The counselor said, "You both have issues."

Why did the cow go to see a psychiatrist?

Why did the witch go to anger management?

The cow was having **moo**d swings.

The witch kept flying off the handle.

Why did the tractor-trailer tire see a therapist?

Because it was under a lot of pressure.

What happens if you're already depressed and then you discover that you put soy sauce in your apple cider?

You get suicidal.

Why did the horse have to go see a therapist?

Because he was so **Neigh**-gative (**Ne**gative).

Patient: Doctor, our daughter won't stop eating cookies!

Dr. Dickens: Well that's crummy.

Why did the crazy psychiatrist prescribe anti-psychotics to his telephone?

To keep it from hearing voices.

Dr. Dickens says to a patient, "Your file here says you're a Kleptomaniac, have you been taking anything for this?"

Why did the undercover officer have to see a vocational therapist?

The police chief kept bugging him.

Patient 1: These side affects are causing severe constipation, sometimes I go two weeks without a bowel movement. It's so bad that I pray to have a bowel movement.

Dr. Dickens: Holy shit!

Patient 2: Doctor these medicines are giving me diarrhea, can you prescribe something for that?

Dr. Dickens: Have you tried anything over the counter?

Patient 2: Well, I took some ginseng.

Dr. Dickens: Ginseng is supposed to help boost energy levels, why would you take that for diarrhea?

Patient 2: I was pooped-out.

Why did the holistic psychiatrist prescribe ginseng to his shrub?

Because it was bushed.

Patient: Doctor I have a nervous tic.

Dr. Dickens: Here are some tranquilizers and a pill cutter, give your little pet bug one-tenth of a tablet every 4 hours.

Patient: No, I mean **my** face tics when I am nervous.

Dr. Dickens: Well stop getting yourself all wound up.

Why did the crazy psychiatrist put Ritalin in his orange juice?

Because the oranges were having difficulty concentrating.

"Doctor, I'm telling you this medication has made me gain so much weight, my calves feel more like cows, my fore arms feel like eight arms, and my ass feels like a donkey."

Why couldn't the severely obese man go into the anorexic ward?

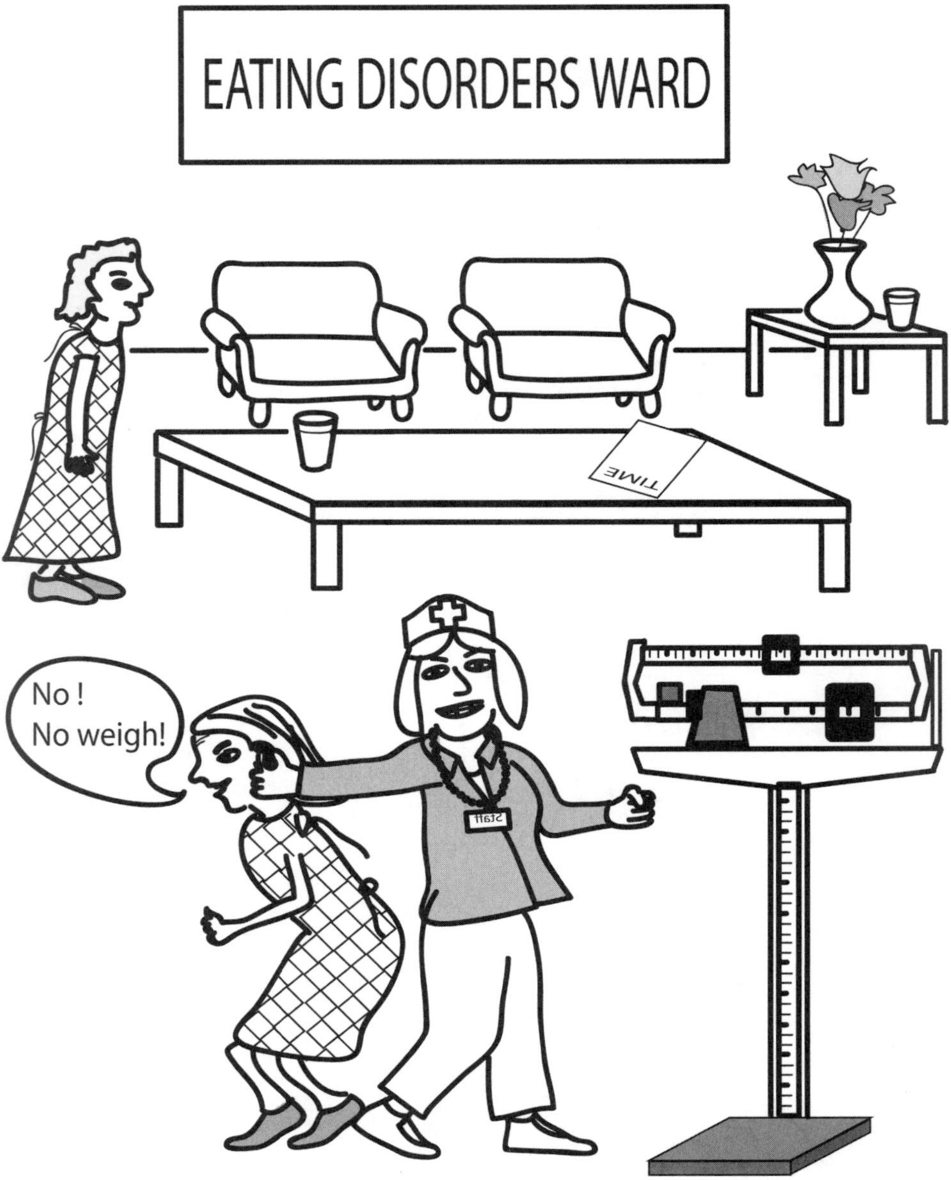
EATING DISORDERS WARD
TIME
No !
No weigh!
Staff

Because he wouldn't fit in.

Why couldn't the boy with pyromania be placed in a foster home?

Because the social workers couldn't find a match.

Guidance Counselor: What would you like to be when you grow up, Jason?

Jason: I'd like to follow in my father's footsteps and be a fire fighter.

Guidance Counselor: Your father's not a fireman.

Jason: I know, he's a pyromaniac.

Why did the Tupperware sales representative wind up in a psychiatric ward?

Because she flipped her lid.

Dr. White: Have you given any thought as to what you would like to be when you grow up?

Allie: Yes I would like to follow in my mother's foot steps and be a disease control specialist for the health department.

Dr. White: Isn't that sweet, you want to be a health care worker just like your mother.

Allie: No, my mother's a prostitute.

What should a depressed person eat for breakfast?

What breakfast food might just fight the blues?

Cheerios.

What **does** a depressed person eat for breakfast?

A depressed person doesn't get up for breakfast.

What does a tribe of schizophrenic cannibals eat for breakfast?

Corny flakes with nuts.

"Dr. Dickens," the secretary hysterically interrupts his session with the cordless phone in her hand, "One of your patients is calling from his cell phone, he says he's on a ledge outside a 14 story building."

"Quick, get me a drink," replies Dr. Dickens.

"What on earth would you want a drink for at a time like this?"

"To take the edge off."

Dr. Dickens goes home and asks his children to pick out some games to donate to the psychiatric institution.

Johnny says, "Take this Chinese Checkers game, it should definitely go to the loony bin, it doesn't have all its marbles."

Jenny adds, "And this jig saw puzzle, it has gone to pieces."

And why did the scrap paper go to the psychiatric hospital?

It felt tear-able.

What did the beads say to the patients in activities therapy?

"We're tired of you stringing us along."

Why did the statue need psychiatric treatment?

Because everyone took it for granite.

In a hospital ward, two nurses talking to each other: "No he doesn't actually have obsessive compulsive disorder, he's still washing his hands because he accidentally touched dog poop during pet therapy."

Why did the macho man wear pink briefs when he was in the psychiatric ward?

Because the staff put his red ones in the wash (pause) and they didn't separate the whites.

Dr. Patall: I got paged while I was at the theater again. Apparently a client thought the distress he felt over his blender breaking warranted an emergency.

Dr. White: After many uncalled-for-interruptions, and a lot of explaining the difference between emergencies and non-emergencies, I finally figured out how to stop my patients from paging me when it's not really an emergency.

Dr. Patall: Please do enlighten me.

Dr. White: I call them back collect.

Why didn't the cold-hearted psychiatrist want his patient to kill himself?

Because then he would be in grave trouble with the insurance company.

Psychic says to customer: I predict you will call me a phony and refuse to pay my fee.

Psychic says to psychiatrist: I predict you will say I am delusional and prescribe me anti-psychotic medicine.

Why did the clone go see a psychiatrist?

Because he wasn't feeling like himself.

Dr. Patall: Have you ever heard the quote 'You can complain because the rose bush has thorns, or you can rejoice because the thorn bush has roses'?'

Patient with Borderline Personality Disorder: I don't like flowers, but I can use the thorns.

Why did the junk man go see a therapist?

Because he was down in the dumps.

How did the pineapple feel when she lost her boyfriend?

Crushed.

Mr. Johns is talking to his female psychiatrist, "I can't take it anymore. If my wife nags me one more time, I'm going to explode!"

"Did you try what we talked about last week?"

"Yeah, yeah, 'I feel angry when you point out my faults.' And I said it as calmly as I could. It didn't work."

"Well Mr. Johns we have been talking about this problem for a year now, and there's only one more method left. But I must warn you it's highly unconventional." She hands him a pocket watch, "whenever somebody is picking on you, you press the button on top, and people stop picking on you within 5 minutes."

Mr. Johns looks at her like she is crazy, but agrees he has tried everything else. He takes the watch home, and his wife begins, "You never help clean the house, and here you are in a messed up shirt, you embarrass me when my friends come over..." Mr. Johns presses the button on the pocket watch and sure enough, within two minutes his wife had calmed down and left him alone.

It worked so well that the next day at work he used it when his boss was picking on him. And within five minutes his boss walked away smiling.

When Mr. Johns goes back to see the psychiatrist he proclaims, "It worked like magic. How is it possible?"

The psychiatrist explains, "When you press the button it sends a tiny electromagnetic pulse through your finger up to your brain, which temporarily paralyzes your vocal cords while causing your head to have involuntary movements in an up and down fashion."

Infuriated, Mr. Johns asks, "You mean this is some sort of shock treatment to get me to shut up and nod!?!" The psychiatrist nods. "I don't need shock treatment for that." He throws the watch down, and abandons the rest of his 45 minute therapy session.

The next evening, the psychiatrist gets a call from a friendly voice, "Hi, this is Mr. Johns. My wife's family is visiting and it turns out, uh, I'm going to need that watch back."

Why did the paper towels have to go see a therapist?

They were absorbing too much crap.

Dr. Dickens asks his famous musician patient, "What made you decide to become a classical musician?"

Patient replies, "My mother told me I didn't know how to compose myself, I showed her."

Why did the train need behavior therapy?

Why did the light rail train need therapy?

The train needed behavior therapy for the same reason why the orchestra needed behavior therapy.

Because they didn't know how to conduct themselves.

And the light rail needed to get back on track.

Why did the microscope need Ritalin?

To help it focus.

5 REASONS WHY YOU SHOULD CHANGE
THERAPISTS AGAIN:

1) When you go in for your 2:00 Tuesday appointment
and the secretary informs you, "Your therapist doesn't
work here on Tuesdays."

2) When your therapist says, "You think you got
problems, listen to this..." and she proceeds to use the
rest of your time telling you how bad she has it.

3) When the secretary announces over the intercom that
her '3:00 is here', and the therapist says "Great, send her
right in", but when you go in she says, "Oh, it's you."

4) When the clock dings she says, "Whew, finally!"

5) When she suddenly blurts out, "You couldn't pay me
$500.00 an hour to listen to this crap!"

Why did the plumber go to a therapist?

Because his life was going down the drain.

Why did the therapist refer the plumber to a drug counselor?

Because she saw his crack.

What did the reformed criminal say to his gun?

"You're fired."

One more reason why you might think about getting yet another new therapist:

You realize you left your hat, so you go back, and as you reach for the door, you overhear her phone conversation, "Oh my God, you wouldn't believe the nut-job who was just here! What am I going to do if she comes back!?!"

Why did the un-embalmed corpse seek therapy?

.

Because he felt rotten.

Why did the mummies go to family therapy?

The father was all wrapped up in himself, the wife was uptight, the children were all wound up, and they were all beginning to crack up.

What famous nursery rhyme character would have made a good candidate for psychotherapy?

Humpty Dumpty, because he cracked up.

Can a cat get Obsessive Compulsive Disorder?

Sure, especially if he is always trying to be purr-fect.

If a person takes their cat to a pet psychologist, does the cat owe anything towards the bill?

Yes, pussy-will-owe.